ORGANIZING YOUR WORK SPACE
A Guide to Personal Productivity

Revised Edition

Odette Pollar

A Crisp Fifty-Minute™ Series Book

This Fifty-Minute™ book is designed to be "read with a pencil." It is an excellent workbook for self-study as well as classroom learning. All material is copyright-protected and cannot be duplicated without permission from the publisher. *Therefore, be sure to order a copy for every training participant by contacting:*

THOMSON
NETg

1-800-442-7477 • 25 Thomson Place, Boston MA • www.courseilt.com

ORGANIZING YOUR WORK SPACE

A Guide to Personal Productivity

Revised Edition

Odette Pollar

CREDITS:
Product Manager: **Debbie Woodbury**
Manufacturing: **Denise Powers**
Designer: **Amy Shayne**
Typesetting: **Fruichantie & Company**
Production Artists: **Nicole Phillips, Rich Lehl, and Betty Hopkins**
Artwork: **Ralph Mapson, Rich Lehl**

COPYRIGHT © 1992, 1999 by Odette Pollar

ALL RIGHTS RESERVED. No part of this work may be reproduced, transcribed, or used in any form or by any means—graphic, electronic, or mechanical, including photocopying, recording, taping, Web distribution, or information storage and retrieval systems—without the prior written permission of the publisher.

For more information contact:

> NETg
> 25 Thomson Place
> Boston, MA 02210

Or find us on the Web at **www.courseilt.com**

For permission to use material from this text or product, submit a request online at www.thomsonrights.com.

Trademarks
Crisp Fifty-Minute Series is a trademark of NETg. Some of the product names and company names used in this book have been used for identification purposes only, and may be trademarks or registered trademarks of their respective manufacturers and sellers.

Disclaimer
NETg reserves the right to revise this publication and make changes from time to time in its content without notice.

ISBN 1-56052-522-3
Library of Congress Catalog Card Number 98-74377
Printed in the United States of America
5 6 7 8 9 10 11 12 GP 08 07 06

LEARNING OBJECTIVES FOR:

ORGANIZING YOUR WORK SPACE

The objectives for *Organizing Your Work Space* are listed below. They have been developed to guide the user to the core issues covered in this book.

The objectives of this book are to help the user:

1) **Manage paper work**

2) **Understand principles of organization**

3) **Learn where items should be kept**

Assessing Progress

NETg has developed a Crisp Series **assessment** that covers the fundamental information presented in this book. A 25-item, multiple-choice and true/false questionnaire allows the reader to evaluate his or her comprehension of the subject matter. To download the assessment and answer key, go to www.courseilt.com and search on the book title, or call 1-800-442-7477.

Assessments should not be used in any employee selection process.

ABOUT THE AUTHOR

Odette Pollar writes the nationally syndicated weekly newspaper column "Smart Ways to Work." She is a nationally recognized speaker, seminar leader, author and consultant to business, government and industry. In 1979, she founded the consulting firm The TMS Group, based in Oakland, California. Odette travels nationally delivering programs which enhance performance, improve office management and streamline day-to-day operations. Her clients include Hewlett Packard, Pacific Bell, Kaiser Permanente, Hitachi, VISA, McDonald's and the Million Dollar Roundtable.

Odette has written four books: *Organizing Your Work Space, Dynamics of Diversity, 365 Ways to Simplify Your Work Life* and *Take Back Your Life.* She is a frequent guest on news and talk show programs addressing the current issues affecting the work place.

In addition to her work with businesses of all sizes, corporations and trade associations, Ms. Pollar consults individually with clients on personal desk management. She shows professionals easy, effective ways to manage time, track projects and activities, simplify paperwork and streamline workflow. Her goal is to help clients regain balance and simplify their personal and professional lives. The systems that she has developed are the result of hands-on experience with clients over the last twenty years.

Ms. Pollar is an active member of the National Speakers Association and the National Association of Professional Organizers.

For more information on how you can arrange for a training program, seminar or personal consultation, please write or call:

Odette Pollar
The TMS Group
1441 Franklin Street, Suite 301
Oakland, CA 94612
phone: 800-599-TIME
fax: 510-763-0790
e-mail: opollartms@aol.com

CONTENTS

CONTENTS (continued)

INTRODUCTION

This is for all of you who, upon scanning the piles on your desk, have said, "I can lay my hands on anything," and then could not. This is for all of you who have just one organizing system called vertical stacking and for others of you who have five, six or perhaps ten separate organizing systems, one for each aspect of your job.

Organizing Your Work Space is for you if:

- You are slowly drowning in a sea of paper.

- The computers in your life seem to be generating more paper than they have eliminated.

- You save most of the paper that crosses your desk because you never know when you will need it again.

- The bulk of your day seems to be filled with shuffling papers, and those papers actually hinder your ability to get other, more important, work done.

- You are overwhelmed and mystified about where to put all the memos, reports, drafts, bills, magazines, correspondence, miscellaneous documents and mail that comes to you.

Being disorganized is like riding a Ferris wheel. There is a sensation of movement, but when the ride stops, you are in the same place you were when you got on. Many people talk about getting organized, but somehow never get around to doing it. Not you. You are ready to tackle the problem head on.

Whatever your challenges in controlling paper, know that you are not alone. In every survey taken over the last twenty years, managing paperwork always falls in the top ten time-wasting activities of managers. Whatever your function—accountant, entrepreneur, administrative assistant, manager, lawyer, executive—this book will help you get organized and stay organized. Through exercises, checklists and easy-to-follow examples, we will help you dig out from under and stay on top of the paper. Section 10 contains checklists and charts for quick review. Use that section for on-the-spot assistance as you work toward mastering your work space.

Good luck as you become more organized!

Odette Pollar

Odette Pollar

PREFACE

Welcome to the revised and expanded *Organizing Your Work Space.* Even with continual advances in technology and computer programs, it seems as though the amount of paper we have to manipulate continues to increase. The need for being organized and having a smooth-running work environment has never been more important. This revised edition includes a section on handling business cards, customizing your personal planner and an entire chapter on dealing with electronic mail.

Learning to manage paper requires motivation, time (to get organized initially) and persistence. Staying organized means that you will have to break some old habits, throw some things away and think differently about saving than you have in the past. Although this can sometimes be frightening, do not let the discomfort stop you. This book will walk you through a very easy-to-use system that will free you from clutter and its companion, stress.

S E C T I O N

1

Why Get Organized?

YES, YOU CAN GET ORGANIZED

"I'll get organized just as soon as I find the time."

"Nobody in my position can get organized."

"I don't know how."

"I have a great system. I just let things go, and if it is really important, someone will call about it!"

"Organized people are boring."

"I'm an artist and creative people aren't organized."

Have you ever heard any of these excuses or used them yourself? Digging out from under and staying on top of the paper in your life is possible. People are not born organized. There is no genetic predisposition toward labeling and classifying systems. Organizing is a skill that is easy to learn.

Clutter is emotionally draining. It makes the amount of work you have to do appear greater than it actually is. Clutter causes work delays, frustration, stress and, of course, loss of time. Arriving at work early Monday morning, prepared to tackle the week and finding yourself facing piles of paper and a completely covered work surface makes you feel tired and irritable. Here you are at 8 A.M. on Monday and already behind. Consider the lost opportunities, the special events you missed because you "stack-filed" the invitations only to find them a week too late.

No matter what your job, no matter how many copies of documents are required by the government or regulatory agencies, no matter how long the sales process takes, you do not have to be inundated by stacks of paper to get your work done.

BENEFITS OF BEING ORGANIZED

Below is a partial list of the benefits of being more organized. Please add as many as you can to this list and check (✔) all that are important to you.

❑　More control over my life

❑　Others can find information when I am away

❑　Freedom from chaos

❑　Be a good role model

❑　Have more time

❑　_____

❑　_____

❑　_____

❑　_____

❑　_____

To be organized is to give yourself more freedom—to have control over the administrative side of your life, to have a greater ability to shift directions without negative consequences. When your life is organized, you can shift directions to take advantage of opportunities without causing a crisis somewhere else. It is actually easier to be organized than to be disorganized, and there is no better time to get started than right now. Your job will not get better, easier or quieter later this week, month or year.

Look at the list you created above. During this cleaning-out process, be sure to focus on the benefits of working smarter. Think about how much better you will feel when you are able to locate items you need the first time you look for them. You will be more comfortable, in better control of your work and will feel less anxiety. Think about the extra time you will have to read those magazines and journal articles you have been keeping. Take control and relieve yourself of the stresses related to being disorganized.

KEY PRINCIPLES

➤ Organization makes your work and life easier.

➤ Organizing is a skill that can be learned by anyone.

➤ Becoming organized is a two-step process:

1. Getting organized

2. Staying organized

The first part of staying on top of the heap involves sorting, tossing and categorizing your papers. The second part is maintenance. Keeping up with your new paper handling and filing system is as important as setting it up initially. The system you establish should be personalized to fit your work needs and your personality while allowing for flexibility. There is no single, perfect process waiting to be discovered. Discard the fear that organized means complicated. Keep your system for tracking papers as simple as possible. Even though getting organized may be something you have dreaded for many months (or even years), it really is not going to take forever!

In tackling an organizing project, keep the following in mind:

• Decide on your goals.

• Realize it cannot all be done in one day, nor should it be.

• Start slowly, one drawer or shelf at a time.

• After completing one section, reward yourself.

• When you get tired, stop.

RATE YOUR SKILL

WHERE ARE YOU NOW?

Rate Your Skills

How do you rate your paper handling and organizing skills?
Place a check (✔) in the appropriate box.

1. Do you have scraps of paper or Post-it®s scattered all over the place with bits and pieces of information noted on them?

    ❏ **Always**   ❏ **Sometimes**   ❏ **Never**

2. Do you tell people not to touch a thing on your desk because, in spite of the apparent mess, you know exactly where everything is?

    ❏ **Always**   ❏ **Sometimes**   ❏ **Never**

3. Do you keep old newspapers and magazines you have not read because there is something very important that you must read in each paper or magazine? Are the stacks growing daily with no real relief in sight?

    ❏ **Always**   ❏ **Sometimes**   ❏ **Never**

4. Do you or your staff spend a significant amount of time nearly every day looking for misfiled or lost papers and documents?

    ❏ **Always**   ❏ **Sometimes**   ❏ **Never**

5. Are there papers in your In Box that have become permanently pending for no particular reason?

    ❏ **Always**   ❏ **Sometimes**   ❏ **Never**

6. Do you often find that a piece of paper filed yesterday is not where you thought it was today and you have no idea where it is?

    ❏ **Always**   ❏ **Sometimes**   ❏ **Never**

7. Have you been putting off organizing your paperwork because you think you are the only one who can do it and you do not have the time to do it right now?

   ❏ **Always**   ❏ **Sometimes**   ❏ **Never**

8. Do you end up saving most of the paper that crosses your desk because you never know when you might need it again?

   ❏ **Always**   ❏ **Sometimes**   ❏ **Never**

9. When you are away, can your associate find a document that you have filed?

   ❏ **Always**   ❏ **Sometimes**   ❏ **Never**

10. Can you easily retrieve information from your files?

    ❏ **Always**   ❏ **Sometimes**   ❏ **Never**

11. Do you have business cards in many different locations in or on your desk?

    ❏ **Always**   ❏ **Sometimes**   ❏ **Never**

12. Do you have equipment, memorabilia and pictures crowding your desk so that you have no room to organize your papers or even to find space to work comfortably?

    ❏ **Always**   ❏ **Sometimes**   ❏ **Never**

Adapted from Stephanie Culp, *Conquering the Paper Pile-up*. Cincinnati Writer's Digest Books, 1990.

S E C T I O N
2

How Backlogs Develop

WHAT IS CLUTTER, ANYWAY?

You are experiencing clutter if:

- Your priority system hinges on the number of coffee cup rings on a piece of paper (indicating how often it has floated to the surface before sinking again).

- Your stacks indicate a priority system where the upper left-hand corner of the desk means something different from the upper right-hand side of the desk.

- Items angled sideways indicate yet another priority.

Clutter is not one project spread out over a work surface. Clutter is unsorted and unrelated documents mixed together. When messages, mail, client files and new assignments all end up in a jumble on your desk—that is clutter. Backlogs develop when you delay in making the decision that would allow the document to continue along its life cycle.

HOW DO PAPER BACKLOGS DEVELOP?

Learning how to prevent backlogs is an important step in staying organized. When a piece of paper crosses your desk, do you ask yourself, "Will I need to refer to this again?" If you answer yes, do you then set it aside because you are not quite sure how to file it and so put it in the To-Decide-Later pile? Are you waiting until you feel in the mood to tackle the item—so it sits over to the side "just for a while"?

It is very helpful to identify the place where your current paper processing system breaks down. Are any of the following true for you? Add your own reasons at the end.

Do you put paper aside when:

❏   You have to wait for a decision or approval before moving forward?

❏   You do not want to or do not know how to respond?

❏   You have a letter that requires a quick response?

❏   You first lay eyes on the document?

❏   You are gone for a few days?

❏   It belongs to a new project and has no existing place in your current filing system? (Is everything a new subject or project?)

❏   You do not have all the necessary information?

❏   You are waiting for a lull in the hectic pace before beginning another large project?

❏   You do not seem to have enough time that day to handle it all?

❏   _____

❏   _____

❏   _____

BLOCKS TO GETTING ORGANIZED

Using the list below, check (✔) the personal challenges you face when you think about organizing your work space. Add additional challenges which block you from getting organized.

❑   No time

❑   Ever-increasing volume of documents

❑   Fear of tossing important paper

❑   No energy

❑   Not sure how to begin

❑   _____

❑   _____

❑   _____

❑   _____

❑   _____

❑   _____

Do not let a prior experience that was not altogether successful cast a shadow over your efforts now. Forgive and forget your past attempts at getting organized. Do not let memories of the time you finally got fed up and forced yourself to sort the entire closet (office, garage, and so on) all in one day stop you. You do not have to wait to start until you are thoroughly disgusted, frustrated, or worse—*mandated* by someone else to get organized.

You can get paperwork under control even though the volume seems to grow every day. The trick is to complete all of the components that a document requires at the right time—before the hour before the absolute drop dead date.

TWO COMMON MENTAL BLOCKS

There are two very common mental blocks that can sabotage your efforts and prevent you from enjoying the benefits of being organized.

1. The Fear of Dumping

Have you ever said any of the following?

"I threw something away once and I needed it again the very next day!"

"What if I get audited by the IRS and I don't have what I need?"

"I'd better keep this because you never know. It might come in handy some time."

"What if I file this material, and then I can't remember where it is?"

"If I leave it out, I can always find it."

We have all had an experience where, once thrown out, an item could have been used again. However, (1) How often does this happen compared with the times items are discarded and never needed again? (2) If you have not organized yourself in a long time and the backlog is severe, you probably would not have found it anyway. (3) Almost everything is replaceable and you could get another copy if you really needed one. (4) What was the consequence of not having the item? If you did not get another copy, then it probably was not worth the clutter it would have caused initially.

Throwing out the excess is not synonymous with destroying your past. You are not erasing the history of your department or that of your company. You are not being asked to live in a sterile, cold, unfriendly environment. You are making a decision about whether an item has enough value to warrant the time, energy and cost of saving it. If not, throw it away, recycle it or, if possible, sell it.

When to Dump

Everything that could conceivably be used in the right circumstances and at the right time, sometime between now and the time you retire, should not be saved. You cannot keep things just because they are interesting. Decide now to make your work space and your life easier by eliminating the excess.

How can you determine what is safe to toss? Here are some guidelines.

➤ Is the information **current** and **relevant** to my work or life?

➤ How **often** will I refer to the information?

➤ Will it add something **new** to the material already on hand?

➤ Do I have the **time** to read this?

➤ Does **someone** else have this information?

➤ How **likely** am I to need to refer to it again?

➤ Is it a **duplicate**?

➤ What is the **date**?

➤ Do I **need** this or simply **want** this?

When to Save

➤ It is the only copy.

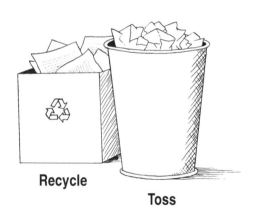

Recycle

Toss

➤ Replication would be very difficult.

➤ You will need to refer to the information again soon.

➤ You are required by law to keep it.

➤ It is an integral part of the client or project file.

➤ You originated the document.

TWO COMMON MENTAL BLOCKS
(continued)

2. The Fear of Becoming Rigid and Inflexible

When you think about an organized person, what image comes to mind? Is it a positive vision? If not, search your underlying beliefs about being organized. Have you ever had a bad experience with a person who was more interested in being neat than in being effective? Does being organized conjure up visions of robots moving about with absolute precision? Are you concerned that getting organized will make you dull, rigid, inflexible (and boring at parties)?

A neat desk is not a sign of a sick mind. Being organized will not force you to keep every paper clip neatly in order. You will not begin to line up files to exactly parallel the side edge of your desk or never have more than one piece of paper on the desk at any given time. Finding something when you need it, quickly, with a minimum amount of anxiety and with confidence that the item will actually be where you look, will not turn you into a "neat-nick."

SECTION

3

Where to Start

DECIDE ON YOUR GOALS

The first step in getting organized is to decide what you want to achieve. As you think about this, consider:

- To what information, materials and supplies must I have easy access?

- How will I be able to retrieve information once filed away in my desk?

- How will I remember to complete unfinished projects once they are put away?

- And, where is all my current work going to be while I am doing this grand organizing project?

List below your specific goals for getting organized. Here are some questions to help you get started. What changes would you like to see happen? What should your new paperwork system accomplish? At the conclusion of this process, what do you want to be different? Please write your goals in the form of positive action statements. For example:

Goals for Getting Organized

❏   I will be able to retrieve information from my files the first time I look for it.

❏   I will be able to empty my In Box in 20 minutes each day.

❏   I will have one location for my project files.

❏   I will have fewer crises in my life from almost missing deadlines.

❏   _____

❏   _____

Keep these goals in mind as you proceed through *Organizing Your Work Space.* All of the procedures and techniques have examples that illustrate the principles. Many have exercises included so that you can practice new techniques.

WHERE TO BEGIN

Look at your immediate work area. Where should you start? It is easiest if you divide the area into sections:

- Your primary desk

- Your support work areas; a credenza; a work station for your computer; a bookcase; a second desk or a work table

- Your personal files

To start the organizing process, choose one section to work on at a time. Begin with the areas farthest away from you for the following three reasons:

1. The items here are probably older and will be easier to make decisions about.

2. You need to make space for other, more appropriate items. Some of what is in or on your primary desk should be moved, and by cleaning the periphery first, you make the necessary room available.

3. You will see immediate results, and that is a good feeling. Seeing progress will motivate you to continue.

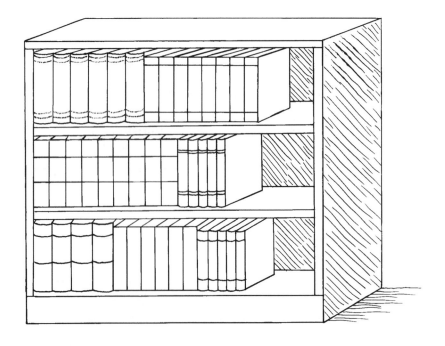

THE BOOKCASES: REDUCE, REFER, REARRANGE

Begin with your bookcases. Plan to spend about one hour on this project. Do not spend more than two hours organizing at one session because it is quite tiring. You are going to be reducing, referring and rearranging all of the items on the shelves.

Touch every binder, book, file and newspaper. Look first to **reduce** by throwing out as much as possible. Dump old versions of manuals, procedures and catalogs. Toss all second, third or fourth copies of items and any information you have not used, forgot was there or is no longer valid. Recycle as much of the excess paper as you can.

   Tip: *You can take everything off the shelves first and reduce, refer and rearrange, as you replace items on the shelves.*

Refer to someone else, information and backup documents for projects that are now within the scope of their responsibility. If you use reference manuals infrequently, send those to a central resource area for your work unit. Move information to the central storage area that you do not need now and do not use but that retains historical value. If you do not have a single, centralized storage location, then box and label the items and move them out of your office. They should be stored somewhere safe, but they should not take up critical space in your office.

Thumb through the remaining manuals to be sure all the information is current. When you do this sorting process, you may find that reducing and referring may take more than one sitting. That is okay. Do not worry about the pile left behind. Simply separate what you have sorted from that which is unsorted. Once the entire bookcase is done, the items that remain must be grouped and **rearranged**.

REARRANGING: HOW TO DO IT

The guiding principle, when sorting, is to put *like things together*. The items on your bookcase will fall into broad categories. Group together all reference manuals, all company information, all vendor catalogs and all reports. If you have attended professional development workshops, dedicate a portion of shelf space to "Training." Place all of those course materials and your notes together. This will enable you to go to one shelf, or one part of a shelf, to find all related items. Books, if in great quantity, can be divided and grouped by subject.

Gather together all loose papers. Add them to appropriate binders. Put those that belong in your filing system in a stack to be filed. (See Section 5.) If the binders become too bulky, divide the information by date, by region or by department.

Three-hole punch miscellaneous information, and arrange it logically in a binder. For example:

- Arrange telephone lists for large companies alphabetically.

- Organize meeting records chronologically.

- Store catalogs or vendor information alphabetically, by subject or chronologically.

- Order marketing prospect call sheets alphabetically or chronologically.

- Collate accounting procedures chronologically.

Label the outside of every binder. Clear labels will make it easier for you and for others to use these resources. Do not rely on your memory. It may fail you, and it makes it impossible for associates to locate documents in your absence.

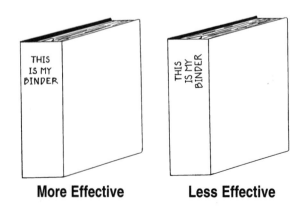

More Effective   **Less Effective**

HANDLING THE EXCEPTIONS

The bulk of the bookcase is arranged. But what do you do with the miscellaneous, weirdly titled, won't stand up alone, and not really large enough for its own binder, type of material? This is still manageable by placing like things together.

Problem

You have attended training courses in stress management, time management, effective selling and interviewing techniques, yet none of them had their own workbooks. You have only notes and a few short articles for each session.

Solution

Place them all in a binder that carries the broad heading "Training." Divide the binder by tabs labeled with each course name and, perhaps, date. This prevents the separate subjects from becoming hopelessly tangled yet still keeps all the information together. Whenever you have miscellaneous training items, just add them to the binder.

Problem

Three years have passed and you now have four binders, all labeled "Training" with mixed subjects inside. Whenever you need to find course notes, you have to page through all four until you find the stress management information.

Solution

When a category becomes too large, and it takes too much time to find particular items, break the group into more specific categories. Take the four binders and sort the contents by placing, once again, like things together. The courses will divide into natural groupings. You may then have binders labeled: *Training-XYZ Company, Training-Management Development, Training-Technical.*

HANDLING THE EXCEPTIONS
(continued)

Problem

You return from a trade show or a conference with stacks of information and literature that you gathered at the booths. You have also been gone three days and so a pile of work faces you when you return.

Solution

Immediately, sort all of the new information. Pull out all that which you know is reference and put it directly in the appropriate subject files. Integrate the remainder into your reading schedule. If there is a large quantity, set aside time on your calendar within a week of your return to sit down and review the information while the context is still fresh.

SUMMARY

Organizing requires set up time and ongoing maintenance. Your new system should be easy to understand. Before you start this project, decide on your goals and remember to reward yourself along the way. Keep these principles in mind:

✔ **Start slowly.**

✔ **Place like things together.**

✔ **Subdivide where appropriate.**

✔ **Feel free to shorten a category, as well as to expand a category.**

S E C T I O N

4

Your Work Area

THE FOGGERTY REPORT, SIR?   IT'S ON MY DESK...
YESSIR, SO IS THE HENDERSON FILE... ON MY DESK...
...UH-HUH, THAT'S ON MY DESK, TOO... RIGHT HERE.
MY DESK, SIR? NORMAL SIZE...WHY DO YOU ASK?

THE CREDENZA

The bookcases are organized. There is some empty shelf space remaining. (This is okay and does not need to be covered with anything!) Extra space allows for future growth. The next area to address, as you clear the way toward your primary desk, is the credenza.

Empty one drawer at a time and wait to tackle the files in the deep drawer until everything else is finished. Place all note pads, Post-it®s and office supplies in one drawer. Place in-house mailing envelopes in another drawer. Keep only one week's supply of envelopes in your desk. If you have dedicated a drawer for items to read, one credenza drawer given over for this purpose is useful. (More information on managing reading is in Section 8, page 76.) Your dictionary, other frequently used reference manuals, logs and directories, would be appropriate on the shelves inside the credenza. Oversized computer printouts, catalogs that need to be closer than your bookcase and some small equipment can also be stored here. Be cautious. Just because it has doors on it does not mean that clutter can hide here.

YOUR DESK DRAWERS

Think of your entire desk as "prime space." Anything that stays this close to you must earn its keep, which means you use it often. Start with the drawers, sorting these as you did the credenza, by consolidating, dumping and rearranging one at a time. Throw away the unused, useless, old or unidentifiable items. This includes the power cords to equipment you no longer have, 150 year-old rubber bands, gadgets that never really worked properly, keys that open nothing you own and business cards that are yellowing around the edges. Consider the six dozen pens and pencils, the four rulers, the three pairs of scissors, the innumerable bottles of white-out, in every color, the 10,000 paper clips that litter the bottom of drawers, not to mention the numerous sticky note pads in every size. Keep only the supplies and quantities you really need and return the rest to the supply room.

As you proceed, take a moment to reflect on why you rent an apartment or own a home. One reason is that it is a place to return all those personal items that have slowly encroached upon your work space. This means that you must limit your personal items to one drawer (no, it cannot be the big file drawer). Take home the extra pairs of shoes, empty food containers and extra clothing. Throw out the plastic utensils, paper bags, mustard packages, congealed sugar, the two-quart bottle of Cremora with two tablespoons left in the bottom. Oh yes, and do something with all those napkins.

As you sort, doubtless you will discover odd bits of interesting information, old cartoons, work assignments, notes on a project or two that you had planned to start when you had time. Take it all out and put it on top of your desk. You will get back to it soon.

EQUIPMENT

The equipment you use regularly should be within easy reach. However, the phone, business card holder, calculator, radio, pen and pencil set, a cup containing miscellaneous pens and pencils, framed photos, In and Out Boxes, a paperweight, not to mention the computer, do not all need to live in the open, crowding your space so you cannot work effectively.

Frequency of use is the key to location. The more you use it, the closer it should be to you. This applies to equipment, files and supplies. Tape and staplers can often live inside the top drawer of your desk without being inconvenient. Pens and pencils are fine on your desktop. But, do you need dozens of each? Move the radio, pencil sharpener and photos to the credenza. Remove the things that make you feel cluttered and give yourself a comfortable working environment.

Ergonomics

Consider ergonomics. Just because the telephone has always been in the right hand corner of the desk does not mean that it should remain there. Consider putting it on a credenza behind you if you do not use it much. Mount it to the wall or place it on a shelf above you if that is more convenient. Consider comfort in addition to ease-of-use for those items that you spend a great deal of time using. Make sure to adjust your chair to a proper height so that work surfaces are comfortable. The chair should also have adjustments for your back. Computer keyboards should be lower than the height of a standard desk. This helps prevent repetitive motion injuries in the wrist and arm.*

* For an excellent book on this subject, read *Productivity at the Workstation* by Robert Regis Dvorak (Crisp Publications, 1990).

THE FILE DRAWERS

Now the drawers are neat, the contents rearranged so that items are placed appropriately, according to use. Lower drawers for personal items, middle drawers for office supplies, note pads and so forth and top drawers for letter-head, envelopes, paper clips, pens, pencils, stapler and tape. Return now, to the deep file drawer in the credenza. The files here are also obligated to follow the principles we have been discussing:

- Sort and consolidate

- Like things together

- Frequency of use

STEP 1

Sort files by use. If you touch them once every three to four weeks, they can remain. If you use them less frequently, move them to the central files. Be rigorous in making this determination, particularly if you are cramped for space. Remember, it takes less time to walk out of your office and down the hall for a file you need once a month than it takes to move the file regularly in order to get those you use more often. Old information or background materials should not take up critical space, forcing you to spread your active files all over because there is no file drawer space available.

STEP 2

Label files by using the subject to which the papers refer as the broad heading. If you find more than one file with related information and it won't be too cumbersome, place all the material in one folder. (We will discuss more labeling principles in Section 5.)

STEP 3

Clean out all remaining files if they are bulky. Papers should not stick out, hide the label on the tab or rub against the top of the drawer. Dump outdated information, copies of drafts, old notes and unnecessary reference materials. In cases where all the remaining information is important but too voluminous, divide out the most current information and keep that handy. Place the balance in central files or in a file behind the first one.

CLEARING THE TOP OF WORK SURFACES

Now that you have made space in the drawers, on the shelves, in the cabinets and on the bookcases in your work area, there will be room to put away some of the items currently covering the other surfaces in your office. You can begin to organize the loose papers that are lying around.

Move now to the top of the credenza or your work table. Much of this paper will be older than what is on your desk and will be easier to make decisions about. Start with one stack of papers at a time. Sort from the top down. Do not move one or two items to see what interesting things reside below. No matter how overwhelming it may seem, all of those loose papers will sort themselves out into logical groupings. Some materials will naturally go with related documents. Some will go into your newly labeled files. A surprising amount will be thrown away because they are no longer relevant or have already been handled. Some will represent projects where the next step belongs to someone else. Be sure to send it along with a note. One or two items will go on your desk because they need to be dealt with immediately. What remains will be projects that are active and you are not sure where to place. Set these aside for now and process them along with the papers on your primary desk.

From here, move on to organize the second desk, if you have one, or computer work station, using the same techniques outlined in this section. If you have a freestanding file cabinet, remember to label the outside of the drawers with your new categories. Sorting the contents of a freestanding file can be done last, after you have finished clearing your desk.

HOW ARE YOU FEELING?

Congratulations on your success! You have come a long way. Did you find the process uncomfortable, or possibly frightening? If so, you are not alone. The process of getting organized and throwing things out can be tiring and filled with anxiety. Be proud that you did it anyway, in spite of the fear. Do not let the emotions stop you from moving forward.

You have now completed the bulk of organizing you set out to do. How does your office look? It should be much neater with fewer papers and miscellaneous objects sitting out. Your books and binders are logically arranged and clearly labeled. The drawers are neat and tidy. The only thing remaining to clear is the top of your desk. The following sections of the book will discuss filing principles, strategies for keeping the desk clean, tools to track delegated work and techniques for maintaining your paper management system.

Please answer these questions.

1. How do you feel about your progress so far?

_____

_____

2. How did you work through the emotions associated with getting organized?

_____

_____

3. Is your organizing moving toward the goals you listed on page 19?

_____

_____

4. What changes have you noticed in your ability to work?

_____

_____

5. What benefits have you experienced so far?

_____

_____

SUMMARY

Start by sorting your bookcases, then your credenza, followed by the drawers of your primary desk. Finally, clear the surfaces of your second desk or work table. Use these principles:

✔ Dump or recycle as much as you can.

✔ Sort and consolidate wherever possible.

✔ Sort files and equipment by frequency of use. The less often touched, the farther away they should reside.

✔ Label all files.

✔ Clean out the contents of individual files, keeping only critical items.

S E C T I O N

5

Filing It and Finding It

COMMON FILING MISTAKES

➤ Not remembering how you categorized something.

   "Now, where would I have put that?"

➤ Creating a good system but not keeping up with it.

   "It works when I use it."

➤ Creating a separate file for every type of document.

   Lots of files with only a few pieces of paper in each one.

➤ Creating files with long, convoluted titles.

   "Samples of How to Contract Work Out to Engineering and Design Drafting Together Plus Three Consultants' Names."

➤ Filing indefinitely. No provision for purging files.

   "We throw nothing away before it's time."

Your personal filing system should be:

✓ **Simple**

✓ **Easy**

✓ **Manageable**

FILING GUIDELINES

Setting up and maintaining files is a very important component to getting organized. Filing is also the area where it is most tempting to throw your hands up in frustration. This section is written in segments, which allows you to locate quickly the parts that will help you. Read the next nine pages. Then, go back and read them again, more slowly, with your files in front of you. Start to relabel your files immediately. As you read, if there is a portion of this chapter that does not apply to your situation, skip it. Once you have enough filing ideas and have developed an effective system, go to page 48, and continue reading with the section called "How to Maintain Your Filing System."

Your Personal Files

One of the most important areas to address in getting your work space under control is your personal files. You need to be able to easily retrieve filed information and have a place to put your loose papers. Ninety-five percent of the time you should be able to go to a single location to find a document. You should rarely have to look more than two places for an item.

Files can be categorized in one of five ways:

- **Subject:** using things or items

- **Alphabetic:** using names or places

- **Numeric:** using numbers

- **Geographic:** using cities, counties, regions, states or countries

- **Chronological:** using dates, the most current in front.

For your personal use, the files in your desk and credenza are, most often, satisfactorily set up using alphabetic or subject headings only. Unit-wide, department-wide or central company files generally use some combination of the remaining three categories.

SETTING UP YOUR SUBJECT FILES

Do you wear different hats in your daily work? Most jobs have an administrative element as well as a larger project component. It is very helpful to establish two types of files that will separate these major components of your work. Start with the following two steps.

STEP 1   Create Working Project Files

These are your action or current project files. They are easy to identify and, probably, already exist in some form. Examples include:

- **Client or customer name** (Pollar, Odette; Crisp, Michael; Hilton Hotels; IBM; Hewlett Packard)

- **Project name** (Customer Feedback; The Annex Group; Unit Replacement; Office Relocation)

- **Course name** (Time Management; Advanced Management Training; English as a Second Language)

- **Contracts** (The Bailey Group; XYZ Vendor)

STEP 2   Create Working Administrative Files

These are your ongoing operational files dealing with administrative activities. These subject files might include:

• Budget	• Staff meetings	• Accounts payable
• Newsletters	• Travel	• Personnel files
• Suppliers	• Marketing	• Accounts receivable
• Vendor files	• Equipment	• Procedures

You will not use every heading listed above. Use those that will hold a quantity of the papers that you deal with regularly.

SETTING UP YOUR SUBJECT FILES (continued)

Tip: Create a Personal File

☛ This file carries your name and is where you place all those things that are of value to you, or pertain to you, and need to be saved. This is where your personal information is filed, such as certificates of completion and accomplishments that would be useful on a resume or biography. This file might also include postcards from friends, restaurant menus and cartoons, but be very selective about what you save.

Tip: Create a Humor File

☛ If your personal file becomes unwieldy because you have kept so many pages of humorous phrases, sayings and cartoons, pull those and create a separate file. Giving them a home means you can easily retrieve them. They no longer float in various locations in the desk, and you can rotate the cartoons that are pinned to your wall.

EXERCISE:

Review the files you have placed in your credenza. (See Section 4 page 27.) Do most of them fall into these three areas? How about those in your desk? Take a moment to add any new headings that you need.

Take a look at your progress. At this point, you should see a significant reduction in the number of loose papers lying about and in the amount of "stuff" sitting out. As you move on to clear the top of your desk, it will be easier to make decisions about where to place documents now that these files have been set up.

FILING PRINCIPLES

PRINCIPLE #1

FILE PAPERS IN THE BROADEST POSSIBLE CATEGORY

Thick files are easier to deal with than thin. Instead of having numerous files with only a few pieces of paper in each one, consolidate all related materials under the most general category that is practical. Notice that the working files we discussed earlier, whether administrative or project, are subject files. They all contain information on the same issue.

Example:

You have information on your company's five-year plan, your department's three-year plan and a copy of your annual goals. Place these together carrying the name of your organization, "XYZ Planning." Then there is only one place you have to look for all company planning information.

Example:

If you have weekly staff meetings but only quarterly department meetings, instead of dividing those into two separate files, consider keeping them together, particularly if the minutes of the department are brief. It is likely that you will need to refer to them during one of the weekly meetings. If combining both sets of meeting minutes does not make the file too bulky, it is easier to house them in a single location. Additionally, this is where you would file items required for the next meeting, such as ideas or suggestions, status updates and any documents that you will use at the next meeting.

MORE PRINCIPLES

FILING PRINCIPLES (continued)

PRINCIPLE #2

HEAD FILES WITH A NOUN

To help make Principle #1 easier, find the key subject area and use that to label the file. The broadest subject is *Staff Meetings*, not *Minutes, Staff Meetings*. The first association in your mind when you want to retrieve information is not that it is a part of the minutes but, rather, that the item was a part of the staff meeting. Avoid labeling a file with a number, date or adjective. Rather than a label reading *How to Negotiate Contracts*, a more effective label, starting with a noun would be *Contract Negotiations*.

EXERCISE:

You are conducting a series of surveys of your customers about your organization's service, quality and perceived value. These quality improvement surveys will be coming in from the entire Western Region.

What are the options for labeling that file?

_____

_____

_____

_____

_____

Did you list any of these options? *Customer Service, Quality Improvement, Current Customer Service Research, Surveys, Western Region Surveys.* The broadest heading is *Surveys.* If you need to break the file down more specifically, then use secondary information in your label, *Surveys-Customer Service*, or *Surveys-Quality Improvement.*

Labeling Exercise

To get some practice in using labeling principles, please write more effective headings for these subject files:

- References on New Boiler Installation _____

  _____

- Updated Mailing List _____

  _____

- Newsweek Magazine _____

  _____

- Macintosh Computer Information _____

  _____

- Articles _____

  _____

- Government Reports _____

  _____

- Copies of Consultant Contracts_____

  _____

- 1992 Operating Plan _____

  _____

- Operations _____

  _____

- How to Write a Company Newsletter _____

  _____

See answers, next page.

FILING PRINCIPLES (continued)

CHECK YOUR ANSWERS

➤ **References on New Boiler Installation:** Head the file with a noun and choose the category it refers to. *Boiler Installation* is the label.

➤ **Updated Mailing List:** *Mailing List* is the subject. *Updated* tells you very little. Updated from when? If you need that information on the label, carry a date as secondary information, *Mailing List, 1998.*

➤ **Newsweek Magazine:** If you are a reporter, if you work for *Newsweek* or need to keep the entire magazine each month, this is the appropriate heading. Remember to clip key articles, mark the date and issue and not save the entire periodical. (Better yet, take magazines out of the files, place them in a magazine holder and store on the bookcase.)

➤ **Macintosh Computer Information:** Okay, as is, if you only have one computer. If you have more than one, the heading should be *Computer Information, Macintosh,* so that *Computer Information, P.C.* and *Computer Information, HP,* are all next to each other in the files.

➤ **Articles:** Articles should be divided out and filed with other materials pertaining to the subject the article refers to. If you keep articles from the *Harvard Business Review, Working Woman* and *Executive Boardroom* on general business skills development, your file might be labeled *Business Practices, General.*

➤ **Government Reports:** Fine, as is, unless that heading is too broad and you have six or eight different reports. In that case, label the file with the specific name of the report. Also, since government reports are rarely individual submittals, most of the people around you participated in the preparation or are aware of the report. This means that the association in everyone's mind is by title of the report, not the specific agency to which it goes.

➤ **Copies of Consultant Contracts:** The broadest category is *Contracts.* However, if the only contracts you deal with are from consultants, label the file *Consultant Contracts.* The secondary heading of *Copies* is necessary only if you need to distinguish it from originals or samples.

➤ **1992 Operating Plan:** Place the date last, *Operating Plan, 1992.*

➤ **Operations:** Good title as is.

➤ **How to Write a Company Newsletter:** The file is about *Newsletters,* so label it that way. It could contain samples of newsletters, ideas for layout, bids on printing costs, etc. Keep the broadest heading possible, for as long as it is practical. (You can drop the company from the title because it is probably implied—what other type of newsletters are you going to be saving?)

FILING PRINCIPLES (continued)

PRINCIPLE #3

ALPHABETIZE

After you have divided your files into broad areas, group each subject area together. Alphabetize within each grouping. This will make retrieval smooth and easy. When adding documents to a file, place the most recent in front. This will save you much searching time, particularly when your file folders have lots of papers in them.

While you are taking the files out to alphabetize them, you should organize the file space so that it is convenient and accessible. It is uncomfortable to twist your body around or get up to see the labels on files that run from the front of the desk drawer to the back. Most standard desk drawers will hold one or two parallel rows of files that face you. The metal divider that holds files from falling over often will serve as the divider between the two rows of files. Hanging files as well as standard manila files should be turned to face you.

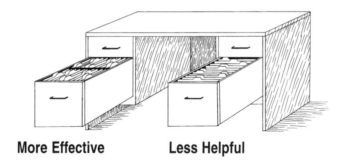

More Effective   **Less Helpful**

PRINCIPLE #4

FILE ARTICLES BY SUBJECT

When you read newspapers, magazine, journals and newsletters and decide to keep certain articles, place those with related information. Notes, articles, reviews and interesting columns are of value because of the subject they discuss. Their content is what matters, not the form. **File all information according how you will use it, not where you found it.** (It is a good idea to note the original source on the article in case you need to give out the reference at some point.)

ADDITIONAL FILING INFORMATION

Heading Files With a Noun-Supplemental

In some instances, when files are very voluminous, you may need additional information in the heading. If it needs a tertiary division, you can break the information down geographically, numerically or chronologically. Thus, *Surveys; Southern California, 1996-1998* and *Surveys; Northern California, 1997-1999.* (Most likely the older survey results would be in a central file location and only a summary would reside in your desk.)

More than One Heading

Here is a tricky situation. What happens when you have an item that can go in more than one location or carry more than one heading easily? To quote *Getting Organized*, by Stephanie Winston, "…Let's say, though, you have stacks and stacks of personal mail to keep—much too much to fit into one folder. Should these folders be labeled *Letters, Susan* or *Susan, Letters*? If the person is the relevant subject, then the folder should be labeled *Susan* or *Michael* rather than *Letters, Susan* or *Letters, Michael*. If Susan or Michael is so important that there's a whole folder's worth of letters from each of them, there will probably be other materials about Susan or Michael that will go into the same folder. In other words, if you ask the question, What is the file about? and the answer is the person, not the letters, then the name should go on the label."

Another illustration:

"Property deed from the lawyer. This could be confusing. Should the deed be filed under the name of the lawyer? Or, supposing this specific property is located in a little town called Eastgate. Again, What is the piece of paper about, in its broadest terms? The answer is Property. Unless you have a great many holdings indeed, the chances are that any correspondence or documents about all of your property will fit in a single folder."

HOW TO MAINTAIN YOUR FILING SYSTEM

1. Keep it simple.

2. File regularly.

3. Keep files lean by purging them frequently of excess information, old notes, and so on.

4. Set up a time, once a quarter or two times a year, to purge files you use infrequently.

5. Do not bother to file every business card you receive, information you have in another form, duplicates, obsolete information, or items other people insist you take.

SUMMARY

Your personal files should be easy to access and enable you to reduce the choices of where a document can be filed. The five principles of filing are:

Filing Principles

✔ **File papers in the broadest possible category.**

✔ **Head files with a noun. Rarely, if ever, start with a date, number or adjective.**

✔ **Alphabetize.**

✔ **File articles by subject.**

✔ **File and purge regularly.**

SECTION

6

Managing Your Desk and Your Papers

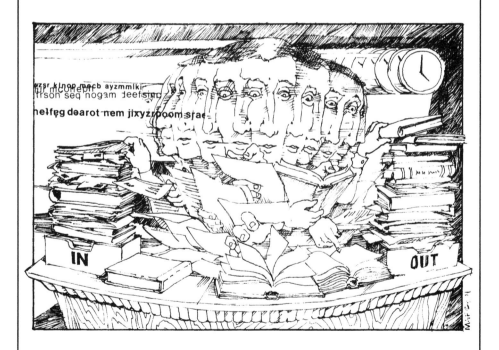

THE TOP OF YOUR DESK

Now, let's move to the top of your desk. Here resides new information, items you discovered as you cleaned out your desk drawers, miscellaneous files, critical items, long-term projects, completed work, phone messages, notes and lots of little pieces of paper in strategic locations about the desk.

There may be documents waiting to go out, items waiting for a return call, tickets for a sporting event three weeks away, a poem written by your niece, a couple of calendars, a sample of a product you may purchase, a pile pending your decision, another pile pending their decision, things to read, a generic sort of aging pile, a funny cartoon and more than one of those neat plastic stacking trays.

The top of the desk should support only the most critical items and information. This is where decision making can potentially break down. The goal is not a spotless desk at all times. Rather, it is the ability to find things when you need them and to always have a clear workspace. You must process everything on your desk by putting it into its proper location quickly and easily. The organizing you did earlier in setting up working files and clearing extra space will come in handy now. First, move as many of the items off the desk as you can.

All the file folders should be put away properly. Older, inactive ones go to storage or central files. Those you use once a month, or more frequently, go to the credenza. Place active files in your desk drawer.

All items waiting to be distributed should be moved off your desk or placed in your Out Box. A firm decision has been made about these items, so they should not remain out and floating around.

 Tip: *Set up an Out Box, if you do not have one. Use it for items going to colleagues, papers to be filed outside of your office, copies to be made and tasks delegated to others. Keeping a "To-File" stack can be more effective than getting up and walking out of your area every time you need to file something. But be wary of letting that pile get too large. Clear the Out Box at least once a day.*

Reading material should be skimmed, and a decision made on the importance of each item. If you will need it in the near future and truly believe that you will have time to read it, then file it (by subject) immediately. Resist the temptation to put it aside for later. Once you have made a decision on any piece of paper, process or file it promptly. (See Section 8 for more on reading material.)

OUT OF SIGHT IS OUT OF MIND

Every document needs a place where it will not be forgotten until the work it represents is completed. So far, you have not filed anything that you are presently working with. Because out of sight often does equal out of mind, much of what remains on your desk is in process in some way. The trick is to put it away, be able to find it again and not forget the next action step. The way to remember is to write things down. If you are likely to forget the next step you must take, then write yourself a note—no, not on a little piece of paper. There are only three places to make these notations:

1. On Your Calendar

2. On Your To-Do List

3. On Your Master List

Then you can keep the documents in the appropriate file.

1. CALENDARS

Keep track of appointments, due dates, project deadlines and meetings on a calendar. It is easy, fast, clear and safe as long as you use only one calendar. Once a calendar becomes unworkable, usually because an aspect of your work becomes more complex than a single calendar will allow, you might consider other options. For example, if you only have two people reporting to you, simply noting due dates on your calendar may be sufficient. However, if you are delegating to five people and managing more complex projects, consider using a Project Monitoring Form. (See page 56 for more on tracking delegated work.) Keep the calendar easily accessible on top of your desk.

Tips for Using Calendars

☞ Use only one. Having two or three means you may forget to transfer information from one to another.

☞ Write down everything that is a firm commitment. Do not trust your memory. Writing it down also enables you to see commitments in relation to one another.

☞ Review your calendar of activities in advance. Check it daily. This prevents surprises.

☞ Choose the type you feel most comfortable using. There are many options, week-at-a-glance, month-at-a-glance, some are pocket-size while others are 10" x 12" folder size. Some people like to have a full page devoted to each day of the week. Others find a compact system more suitable.

☞ Consider a calendar that has sections for notes, telephone numbers and projects.

☞ Write everything in pencil.

OUT OF SIGHT IS OUT OF MIND (continued)

2. DAILY TO-DO LISTS

A To-Do List is a way to keep track of tasks that can be completed in the next one or two days. You should not have more than fifteen items on it. This list should serve the following purposes by helping to:

- Remind you of things you are likely to forget (it is not a listing of everything you do each day).

- Set priorities based on importance, not just on urgency.

- Plan, because you can estimate how much time each item will take.

- Regain your focus after being interrupted.

Example:

Priority	TASKS	Time
B	*Review minutes of department meeting*	
C	*Call Roger re: equipment*	
A	*Straighten out Anderson invoice*	
B	*Set up meeting with Bud, Jorgé, Marilyn*	
A	*Set up interview with new vendor*	

Use a standard sheet of paper for your list and keep it readily available for quick review. (Many day planners have a place for this list. See Section 9 for more about using these systems.) Have only one To-Do List going at a time. Be sure that you do not place too much on it initially. A two-page list is entirely unrealistic. If your list becomes cumbersome, if you never seem to be able to get through it in less than a week or you find yourself continually rewriting items, take a moment to review the proper uses of a To-Do List. If the items you find yourself transferring over and over again are large or time consuming, using a separate Master List may be helpful for you.

3. MASTER LIST

A Master List is helpful if you have:

- Quarterly or semi-annual projects to complete that you may not start immediately or work on daily (be sure to write their due dates on your calendar)

- A number of things to do that are pending production and do not have a file because no other supporting materials yet exist

- A bulletin board on which to post it as a reminder of the big picture

Example:

Priority	PROJECTS	Due Date
A	Check copyright dates on all workbooks	6/15
B	Expand newsletter from 4 to 6 pages	8/30
A	Investigate new phone system	5/5

Separating daily activities from long-term projects is helpful because you will not have to keep rewriting the bigger projects every day. Also you can place one task on the daily To-Do List, for example, to create a written plan of attack for one of the larger long-term projects. When you put something away, if you plan to continue to work on it during the next couple of days, note the next step on your To-Do List. List it on your Calendar if it carries a specific due date. If it is a new assignment or an opportunity to pursue, put it on your Master List.

A DAILY TO-DO LIST IS...	*A MASTER LIST IS...*
- Rewritten or added to many times a day	- Something that grows slowly and is not added to daily
- Filled with quick items	- Filled with longer, bigger tasks
- Out on your desk for quick reference	- Often posted on the wall as a reminder

TRACKING DELEGATED WORK

If you delegate regularly and, therefore, need to remember who you asked to do what and by when, a separate tracking tool for work assigned to others can be helpful. This **Project Monitoring Form** is one of the pieces of paper that can and should remain out on your desk.

The **Title of Task** column requires only enough information for you to understand the assignment. **Delegated To** should carry the person's first name or initials only, whichever is fast and recognizable. The **Date Given** and the **Due Date** columns are the key to staying on top of the work. Filling these in when the assignment is given removes any ambiguity on your part and on theirs. The **Status Check** date refers to a time or times when you want to be informed of the progress of the work. This lets you know the assignment has not been forgotten by the other person and eliminates your need to ask them every other day, "How's it going?"

The final **Comments** column allows you to make notes about the performance of the work—was it received on time, early or late, and how complete was the job and other relevant information. You can later refer to these notes when it is time to write performance reviews. This gives you timely, accurate performance information as it happens so that the review is based on a history of performance, not only on recent memory.

When using this form, fill all of the lines before starting another page. Do not use separate sheets for each person. It is too cumbersome. Since most delegated assignments are known to other team members, you can post this list if appropriate. It helps everyone understand each other's workload. (Do not fill in the **Comments** column if you are making it public.)

PROJECT MONITORING FORM

Project Monitoring Form

Title of Task	Delegated To	Date Given	Status Check	Due Date	Comments
3 bids on phone system	Bob C.	2/15	3/3	4/1	Project finished early. Thorough work, good recommendations.
Interview vendors for training	Ann T.	3/1	4/15	6/15	Project one week late due to illness, good decision grid, excited about the opportunity.

©1989 Time Management Systems

TRACKING DELEGATED WORK
(continued)

This Project Monitoring Form will allow you the freedom to put the papers related to a project away and not worry that once out of sight it will be forgotten. You have three options for where to file project documents and information.

1. The first and best choice for filing is always to place materials relating to the same subject together.

2. If there is no existing file for a new project and if you delegate regularly to the same people, you might choose to add files to your personal drawer that carry the names of the people you delegate to regularly. All information and projects that involve them would remain filed there until the project is complete.

3. The final option on where these papers can stay is in a Tickler File (See Section 7 page 66) to be pulled up the day before the status check date or the due date.

SUMMARY

The top of your desk should be free of clutter to allow you to work efficiently. Here is how to clear it:

Managing Your Desk

✔ Move all files to their proper locations.

✔ Distribute all materials that go to others, to file or to storage.

✔ Skim reading items and decide whether to keep or not. If you keep it, file it immediately with other related materials.

✔ When you put things away, place a note on your

  • Calendar

  • To-Do List

  • Master List

✔ Use a Project Monitoring Form to keep track of delegated assignments.

SECTION

7

Clearing Off the Stacks

TYING UP LOOSE ENDS

So far you have put away all the file folders, distributed items to others and decided on which reading items to save. Now, return to the top of the desk. What remains?

➤ **Loose papers indicating long-term projects or assignments**.
These get handled very easily. If the paper is related to a subject file that exists, put it away now. If there is no file and the project will grow, then start a file now. Make a note concerning your next step on your calendar or on the Master List.

➤ **The stack of items that is waiting for other people to decide.**
These get handled one of two ways:

- If the return call or fax will happen before the end of the day and you will be finished with the item, then it can remain on your desk.

- If, however, the response will not be quick, the item has been sitting out for a while or, after the information you are waiting for arrives, it still requires more effort on your part, then make a note on your To-Do List and put the balance of the papers in the file. (Remember: File in the broadest possible category.)

➤ **Lots of little pieces of paper.** Throw some away, of course. Record all appointments on your calendar. Integrate into your To-Do List those tasks that can be accomplished in the next couple of days. Transfer notes about work assigned to others onto the Project Monitoring Form. In the future, write notes in the appropriate place initially. For instance, place them on the inside cover of the file folder, on the bottom of client correspondence, or on an internal memo form. Break the habit of writing things down on miscellaneous bits of paper.

TYING UP LOOSE ENDS (continued)

➤ **Things you do not know what else to do with but think are interesting anyway.** In the administrative section of your desk drawer, where there are files containing company information, benefits, meeting minutes, the annual operating plan and so forth, you should have a file that carries your name. This is where you place things only of interest to you. This would include your performance evaluations, your resume, the recipe for Mrs. Field's cookies, the poem by your niece, a cartoon, the copies of the article you wrote for the local news paper, restaurant menus and so forth. Tickets for an event you will be attending might reside here, with a note in your calendar on the date of the event. Be cautious that your personal file does not grow unchecked and become a clutter or a junk file. As with your other files, purge it of outdated material regularly.

➤ **A pile of papers pending your decision.** This may be the most challenging. If you cannot make a decision because of a legitimate need to wait, those papers can be placed in a Tickler File. If the number of items that fall into this category are small, say three or four, there is no reason to set up an entire Tickler system. Simply place those items in a Next-Week file. The remainder of the papers are simply waiting for a decision on your part. There is no additional information required. You are at a crossroads. If you do not decide right now, you create a pending stack. If you decide and put it away, you will break through to the other side and be clearly on the path to better organization.

BUSINESS CARDS

Business cards seem to accumulate rapidly. When you were sorting the desk, did you find some in the upper right hand desk drawer, some in the center pullout drawer and some rubberbanded in the upper left-hand drawer? Keep in mind that business cards, like any kind of information, are only useful if they are retrievable. One of the best things to do initially is to reduce the number that come in. Do not feel obligated to save each one given to you. Only retain those you are likely to refer to again.

When you are handed a card write directly on the card what you are going to do with it or the promise you made. This makes filling the request much easier when you are back in the office.

 Tip: *If you ever jot notes to yourself on the back of your own business card, draw a line through your name across the front of your card. This prevents you from ever giving out a card that contains an important number on the back.*

Store cards in a rotary file or a card file. You can alphabetize these by the name of the company or by the name of the person. Choose whichever way you are likely to remember the person. You can have some filed by company names and some by the person's last name in the same file. If you have two distinct function areas in your job you may decide to use two different card files. For example, one would just be your vendors and the other would be for the remaining cards. This is helpful in instances where integrating the cards would be confusing or retrieval too time consuming.

There are software programs that will allow you to scan business cards and place the contact information into an electronic address book or contact management system. This is a good option if you have hundreds of cards to manage and are very comfortable using a computer-based system.

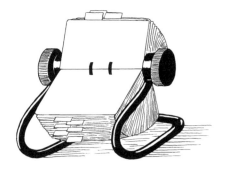

Rotary File

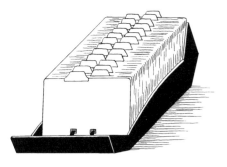

Card File

TICKLER FILES

These are files that provide you with a reminder of what needs to be done on specific days. These files are particularly helpful in jobs where there is a high volume of follow-up activity that must be done on specific dates. Situations that benefit from a Tickler File include sales positions, bookkeeping and bill paying functions and insurance agencies, which must keep track of policy renewal dates.

To establish a Tickler File, set up a series of files numbered *1* through *31*. Follow these by twelve files labeled *January* through *December*. Any item due on a date this month gets filed behind the specific date. Anything due in upcoming months gets placed in the appropriate month's file.

At the end of each month, take the following month's file and distribute all items into the specific date files. An item due on the 5th of September would be in the September file until the end of August. On September 1st, take all of the September items out and place them, accordingly, behind the days of the current month.

This is an excellent system if you have a large volume of items to track. But the only way the Tickler File works is if you check the file every day. Doing this as the first action of your day will help you plan your time and insure that nothing critical slips by undetected.

THE NEXT-WEEK FILE

If you do not have many items, then a Tickler system may be too complex. Instead, label a file *Next-Week* and place all future items that:

- Do not have broader subject files

- Are one-time events that do not rate their own folder

For easy access, place this file in the front part of your file drawer. At the start of each week, review the items and place those you will begin on your To-Do List. A Next-Week file is not cold storage or a place for things not yet decided. When you find yourself asking which Monday it is, or if the file becomes thick with all kinds of papers, then you are not using the Next-Week file effectively. Purge and organize the material regularly.

ODDS AND ENDS

Look back over the last two sections. You have moved most of what has been laying about. Is there anything remaining that does not seem to fit anywhere? Here are a few miscellaneous items and recommended storage places.

ITEM	LOCATION
Instruction manuals	Create a file for *all* equipment instructions.
Extra office supplies	Credenza or back to storage.
Framed photos	Mount on the wall or take home.
Forms: tuition reimbursement word processing supply requests section invoices	Create a *Forms* file. Separate the different forms you use with tabs. Place in the administration area of your working files.
Cute sayings or quotes	Limit two to a wall. Toss others, or place in personal file. (Beware of visual clutter.)
Your company's promotional materials	Paperweights, clocks, and so on. Keep on credenza and rotate when new ones arrive.

MAINTAINING YOUR ORGANIZATION

Part 1: Processing the "In Box"

Keeping the stacks of paper down can be challenging. Work assignments, projects and mail can all arrive when you are not prepared to work on it. Use the In Box as the single place for people to place new information. Processing new work from the In Box each day (or sometimes two or three times a day), should never take more than fifteen minutes. Processing means sorting, deciding and putting away the physical paper even when you have not completed the work the paper represents. You can put anything away when you can answer these three questions.

Three Key Questions

1. What does this refer to?

2. What is my next step?

3. What would I decide if it was one week before vacation?

What does this refer to tells you the subject and therefore the file it should reside in. Keeping all related papers together is a good strategy.

What is my next step tells you where to write yourself a reminder note. When you put work away be sure to place a note on your To-Do List, Master List or Calendar.

What would I decide if it was one week before vacation? Are you more decisive in clearing your desk before a big trip? Why wait to move those papers along? Make your decision as soon as it arrives.

Managing incoming information can be quick and easy when you can remember to use these three questions.

MAINTAINING YOUR ORGANIZATION (continued)

Part 2: Keep the Stacks Away

Now that you have worked hard to get organized, you must keep the stacks from reforming. It is vital that you keep up your new, good habits. To stay on top of the daily papers that will accumulate, you have two options:

1. **At the end of each day,** spend fifteen minutes and clear the top of your desk. This is the best way to stay ahead. One day's accumulation is easily handled.

2. **Spend thirty minutes** twice a week clearing the desk. Under no circumstances should you spend days at your desk and not take a few minutes to clear it off. Remember how quickly the piles will grow.

Part 3: Establish Good Paper Management Habits

➤ Decide now. Ask yourself three questions when you pick up a paper:

   1. What does the item refer to?

   2. What category should it belong to?

   3. What is the next step I must take?

➤ Throw away or recycle as much as possible.

➤ Be very selective about what you keep.

➤ Process each item as soon as it comes in. Do not let the piles multiply.

➤ Put things away. Always refile things quickly.

➤ Keep loose papers to a minimum. Do not keep notes on little pieces of paper.

➤ Set aside time daily to handle paperwork.

➤ If you put something away and you must remember your next step, write a note on your To-Do List, Master List or Calender.

SECTION

8

Managing Your Mail and Your Reading

SORTING INCOMING MAIL

Incoming documents arriving either from internal sources or external mail deserve special attention. While standing at your mailbox, cubicle or central distribution and pick-up area, do an initial screening. Throw away or recycle as much as possible prior to returning to your desk. This is the time for ruthlessness. Most non-first-class mail is junk. How likely are you to need this information?

What remains should be sorted into logical divisions. You have three options for sorting incoming mail: (1) by priority (2) by action or (3) by date.

Sorting by Priority

Divide your incoming documents into A, B, C and D folders.

➤ **A** items are high value and must be done today.

➤ **B** items are also high value but have a longer lead time, often three or four days.

➤ **C** items are less important. They may or may not have a deadline attached. Some of these items you will do and some can be given to others to handle. Some will die a natural death.

➤ **D** items are to file or distribute.

Dividing by priority tells you which items are the most critical. These four groups of documents are then integrated into your work schedule. The A items will be completed by the end of the day (sometimes before noon). The B items are worked next and C's are fit in as time allows. The fourth group, the D's, get distributed or delegated immediately. This system is very useful for jobs that have a high percentage of tasks that require a quick turn around and are time sensitive.

SORTING INCOMING MAIL
(continued)

Sorting by Action

Putting like things together works well with incoming mail. All items requiring the same kind of response can be sorted and placed together. Possible divisions include:

- To-Write or dictate a response (first draft of a proposal, response to a complaint, exit interview, case summary)

- To-Sign (checks, time cards, expense vouchers, final copies of correspondence)

- To-Do today (all items that don't have a subject file and that will definitely be completed by the end of the day)

- Research (large project, history of a situation, an issue to discuss with other people)

If you have an assistant who handles your mail first, this sorting process should be done before you receive the mail. Once an initial decision has been made, whenever you touch this file you know what type of action will next be required.

You should integrate these four groups of documents into your schedule. The writing or dictating group will require some concentration and time. The To-Sign items can be done in between other activities, or while on hold on the phone. To-Do today items are added to your To-Do List and worked according to their priority. Items from the research pile often become projects and therefore earn a file folder and a notation on your Master List.

Sorting By Date

Mail can also be sorted using time as a criteria. This is useful for date sensitive tasks that do not have subject files or another logical place to reside. Use four folders with the following titles: *To-Do Today*, *To-Do This Week*, *To-Do This Month*, *To-Do Next Month*.

Items are sorted based on when you plan to respond. This system works very well for high-volume jobs where routine contacts need to be made such as prospecting and outreach.

The advantage of sorting your incoming mail immediately by priority, by action, or by date is that you have made a firm decision and now know what your day holds. Whichever sorting system you choose, there should be no need to touch the file again until you are ready to complete the work.

IMPORTANT: Choose only one of the three techniques above.

Sorting Mail
Checklist

☑ **Toss out or recycle as much as you can before going to your desk.**

☑ **Make a firm decision, immediately, about what remains.**

☑ **Divide mail into categories by priority, by action, or by date.**

☑ **Once sorted, touch the file only when you are ready to work on the items it contains.**

MANAGING THE READING

After you set aside the To-Read items during the sorting process, you are still left with magazines, professional journals, newsletters and the like. These can rapidly grow out of your reading drawer, cascade down the side of the desk and finally end up residing in stacks and boxes. So much information is available and so much is interesting that it is easy to become overwhelmed.

Evaluate the publications you receive by asking:

- "What would happen if I did not get it?"

- "How often does it offer something genuinely useful, not just interesting?"

- "Which of the periodicals that I actually read offer the most useful information in the best form?"

There is good news and bad news to this story. The bad news is that if this has been out of control for a while, there is no way, short of a leave of absence, that you will be able to read your entire backlog. If it has been sitting for six months or longer, throw it out. In spite of the fear of not being caught up with the latest information, the truth is that you have survived quite well to this point without it. If it gets any older, when you do find time to read it, it will have become history. Reading piles do not age gracefully. They serve no purpose remaining unread, collecting dust and making you feel guilty.

The good news is that you can read some of it. There is a way to keep the stacks of reading down and stay current on key events in your industry. When you sit down to sort the reading file, you must make decisions about (1) how likely you are to read it and (2) how important the information is.

There are four actions you can take when processing the reading stack:

> **1. File the information with related material, unread.**
>
> **2. Read it and file it with related information.**
>
> **3. Route it to someone else.**
>
> **4. Throw it away.**

1. File the Information with Related Material, Unread

It generally takes too long to read everything in depth when it first crosses your desk. So, as you sort through the In Box, skim, clip and file. Place as much reading as you can with its related material immediately.

Example: At the last staff meeting a new project concerned with establishing flexible work time was discussed. There will be many documents coming to you over the next two or three months as this project takes shape. When you notice an article in the Harvard Business Review on how the top three engineering firms implemented flex-time, cut it out and place it immediately in the file. When you have gathered all your information and are ready to write a report, then take the time to read it fully. Many of your reading items can wait safely in this manner.

2. Read It and File with Related Information

If the material to read is short, then read it and decide (1) what it concerns and (2) where it should best be filed. If its proper place is in one of the files in your desk, put it away immediately. If the file is away from your work area, place it in the Out Box and file it when you distribute the contents of your Out Box.

3. Route It to Someone Else

Routed items, reports and catalogs often get sent to the wrong person. When this happens, identify the correct person who may need the information and route it accordingly. (Routing is not meant to overwhelm someone else or to intentionally delay work you should be doing.) Attach a note indicating who it is from and action to be taken.

4. Throw It Away

Of course, what needs to happen to most papers is to throw them out.

MANAGING THE READING (continued)

Unfortunately, there will never be a time when the phone stops ringing, you are entirely caught up, there is no afternoon meeting and you will have three or four hours to just read. In spite of being busy, set aside time on your calendar to read and do it. You may have more to read than one hour a week will accommodate. However, some reading is better than none. This extra time, along with taking reading with you while waiting for appointments, when traveling and during commutes, will help you manage the reading stack. If you can read thirty minutes each day, it would be even better.

☞ **Tip:** *As reported in <u>INC. Magazine</u>, August 1988, Stew Leonard, owner of the largest dairy store in the U.S.A., has come up with a solution for keeping up with his voluminous business book reading list. As Leonard reads useful texts, he underlines passages and scribbles notes in the margins. When Leonard is done, his secretary types up everything marked and the result is a twenty or thirty page summary. This is better than anything he could buy because he has personalized it to his business. Leonard does not need to re-read a 300 page book and his staff is more likely to read his summary than the entire book.*

MORE READING TIPS ⟩

Reading Tips

☞ When reading, highlight passages as you go. This assists you when you are reviewing the information later, and it is helpful to others reading the material after you (perhaps at your recommendation).

☞ Clip articles, note the source and throw the rest of the periodical away. Do not read an interesting article and then set it aside, promising to cut it out later. What that produces is two piles—the original reading pile and another pile containing things you know you need to keep but now have to re-read to remember why you saved the magazine initially.

☞ Read the conclusion or recommendations section first. Go back to the text for details only if necessary.

☞ For long documents, use spot reading. After reading the recommendations or conclusion sections first, look for the purpose of the document by reading the subject line. Note headings, captions, notations under charts, graphs and first sentences of each paragraph.

☞ Read while commuting, waiting for appointments, or on plane trips.

☞ Set aside thirty minutes, at least two times a week, to read. Schedule it on your calendar if you need a reminder. Remember that getting the critical reading done is better than doing none at all.

Managing E-Mail and Personal Organizers

MANAGING E-MAIL

There are many benefits to electronic mail (e-mail). It can improve productivity and increase communication speed. It allows for wide distribution with the push of a button. Distance is no longer a barrier. E-mail is less expensive than the traditional letter when you consider the time to type the document, proof it, address the envelope, stamp and mail it. There is a downside to e-mail, however. This wonderful breakthrough can be a source of distraction and frustration, especially for those who get upwards of 100 e-mail messages a day. When added to the fax, telephone, voice mail, pager, traditional mail and overnight services, there are now so many communication channels that communication is actually hindered. Problems can also occur when people do not receive adequate training in how to use and manage e-mail effectively.

Cautions

Electronic mail is not a secure or confidential medium of communication. Within corporations, having a private password is not guarantee of confidentiality. Ultimate ownership of the equipment, and therefore the messages sent on that equipment, often belongs to the company. Even erased messages can be retrieved from automatic daily backups. The 1986 Electronics Communications Privacy Act in the United States ruled that employers are entitled to read and monitor their employees' electronic mail. Recently, a government employee who used the internal mail system to distribute a questionable document discussing Ebonics was fired. Avoid anything that can be construed as contributing to a hostile work environment.

Send personal messages only if your organization allows it. It is very easy to make a mistake and send a private message to everybody on your list. Electronic accidents can have repercussions far and wide. There have been news reports of department heads accidentally sending staff salary information to everyone on the organization's distribution list. Once sent, it is very difficult and often impossible to retrieve. After your message is in someone else's hands, you have lost control of how it may be further distributed.

For safety's sake, never send a message that you would not be comfortable sending to your parents. Do not send questionable jokes or stories. Those too can cause grief.

MANAGING E-MAIL (continued)

When emotional, avoid sending an e-mail. Emotions do not travel well in written form. Tongue-in-check comments, humor or sarcasm, might not come across in an e-mail message, resulting in misunderstanding and confusion. If you write a response when you are disturbed or angry, wait at least twenty-four hours before sending it. When you read it again, you will probably edit it.

Attachments can be an additional headache. There are many different e-mail and word processing programs in use. It is very difficult to know if recipients have the same software and version that you do. If they do not, it is possible that they will be unable to open and view the attachment. You may be better off simply pasting the message into the body of your e-mail correspondence. Although it may lose some formatting features, the content should be readable. This saves you from having to re-send the item.

Etiquette

Most companies have their own e-mail code of conduct. Ask for any written rules or guidelines, and follow them. Lawsuits have been based on the contents of e-mail messages. General etiquette rules include:

- Ask permission before forwarding anyone else's message.

- Send only to people who really need the information.

- Indicate the priority level of your outgoing messages.

- To help the reader set priorities and manage his or her mailbox, always complete the subject line in the heading, keeping it short and to the point. The more specific you can be, the better. "Project report" is helpful, but "revisions of Anderson project 6/15" is better.

- Copy the sender's message in your reply. If you fail to do so, the sender may forget which question you have just answered, particularly if it is a long communication string.

E-Mail Tips

☞ Screen your incoming e-mail messages by using the subject line.

☞ Use folders to organize messages. Handle these as you do other mail: sort and set priorities on it immediately. The folders will carry the same names as your files because you are dealing with the same issues.

☞ Set specific times during the day to respond to e-mail messages.

☞ To avoid distraction, turn off the audio alarms or visual signals that alert you when a new message arrives.

☞ Do not be seduced by the ease of e-mail. If you would not send it manually, it probably does not need to be sent electronically. E-mail is not automatically more important than other forms of communication.

☞ Discover how the software can be customized for your use. Learn how to set up distribution groupings, reply buttons and a signature file. (A signature can be set up to appear automatically at the end of your message and is useful for promotion or to provide full contact information to the receiver.) You may be able to instruct your system to routinely check for mail at specific times.

☞ If the subject of your reply has changed from the message originally sent to you, change the subject line.

☞ If you are answering a portion of the incoming message, copy that portion into your reply with intent marks (>) or brackets to identify it. This precludes the sender receiving a message that says only "yes, let's do it" and not being sure what "it" refers to.

☞ Keep your messages concise.

☞ Get off routing lists for information that carries no interest.

DAY PLANNERS AND PERSONAL ORGANIZERS

What They Do

Planners and organizers are simply tools to help you manage your life and career. The more complex and demanding your life and work, the more time management tools can help you track the details. There are many choices from paper-based calendars and notebooks to hand-held electronic systems. Find one that suits your current situation. In five years your needs may change and the planner that works so well for you now may need to be adapted or eliminated entirely. Planners and organizers are coming into widespread use. Some of the popular paper-based systems include: Franklin Day Planner, Day-Timer, The Personal Resource System, Geodex Systems and Day Runner, to name a few.

Things to Keep in Mind When Choosing a Paper-Based Planner

Organizers help professionals manage time, information and planning. A good system combines both long- and short-term planning options. This allows you to review major events throughout the year with more specific information month to month. For short range planning, there should be pages that present the entire week or separate pages per day.

Consider the size of the planner and its portability. They range in dimensions from a 4" x 8" all the way up to 8-1/2" by 11". There should be enough space for you to write comfortably. Smaller planners are easier to carry inside of a brief-case or a jacket pocket. Some planners are self-contained units, designed to be used as a briefcase and carried on the shoulder with a strap.

Selection Criteria
- Size
- Features
- Portability
- Looks and Appeal

Organizers incorporate sheets for planning, scheduling, To-Do lists, goal worksheets, note pad, record-keeping tools, yearly projections, Master List and telephone directories. Often other special compartments are provided for credit cards, writing implements and calculators. Some have even more options. Select a system that is as simple as possible, yet meets your requirements. It is tempting to purchase the deluxe model of the item which may have too much in it.

The very first thing to do is customize your planner. Remove any sections that you will not be using. Rearrange the remainder so that the sections you need more frequently are in front and easy to get to. Do not be constrained by any pre-printed tabs and labels that may have come with the system. Feel free to rename the existing sections with headings that make more sense to you. If you need a new section, add it.

Organizing systems are very personal. Take the time to find one that appeals to you and fits in with your style and work responsibilities. The most important thing is to be comfortable and use the system regularly. If you have one that you are comfortable with and everybody else in your new work group uses a different system, resist the to pressure to change. So long as you are meeting your deadlines and not causing compatibility problems for others, keep what works well for you.

Planner Tips

☞ Keep it simple.

☞ Stop using a tool that you have outgrown.

☞ Customize the system using your own headings.

☞ Remove components that you do not use.

☞ Adapt as your needs change.

SUMMARY

E-mail and day planners are tools to assist you in working smarter. Here are tips to keep them under control.

E-Mail Tips

☞ Screen incoming messages.

☞ Do not save or print all of your messages.

☞ Set specific times of the day to respond.

☞ Keep your outgoing messages concise.

Tips for Day Planners and Personal Organizers

☞ Use only one system.

☞ Customize the system using your own headings.

☞ Remove components that you do not use.

☞ Adapt your system as your needs change.

SECTION

10

Quick Review, Charts and Checklists

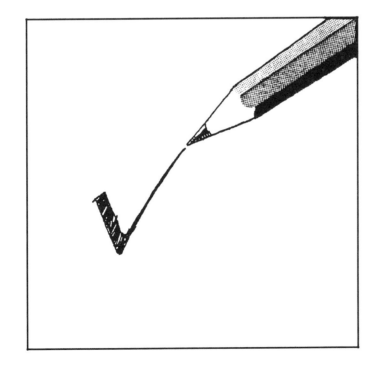

REVIEW: GETTING ORGANIZED FROM A TO Z

Getting Started

What to do:

- ❑ Step 1. Decide on your goals for this project.

- ❑ Step 2. Start slowly, one drawer or shelf at a time.

- ❑ Step 3. Begin by organizing the areas farthest away from your primary desk.

Things to remember:

- It cannot be done all at once.

- Acknowledge your progress as you work.

- When you get tired, stop.

The Bookcases

What to do:

- ❑ Step 1. *Reduce* as much as you can by dumping or recycling.

- ❑ Step 2. *Refer* items to other people, where possible.

- ❑ Step 3. *Rearrange* the remaining items.

Things to remember:

- Put like things together.

- Place bulky items into binders.

- Label all binders.

REVIEW: GETTING ORGANIZED FROM A TO Z (continued)

The Credenza

What to do:

- ❑ Step 1. Empty one drawer at a time and toss or return excess items to the supply room.

- ❑ Step 2. Place less frequently used equipment inside.

- ❑ Step 3. Check that up-to-date and appropriate reference manuals are located on the shelves.

Things to remember:

- • Wait to tackle the file drawer until all others are finished.

- • Be sure to arrange everything in the credenza. Do not let clutter hide here.

Your Desk Drawers

What to do:

- ❑ Step 1. Rearrange contents, placing like things together.

- ❑ Step 2. Limit all personal items to one drawer.

- ❑ Step 3. Put any work-to-do on the top of your desk for immediate processing.

Things to remember:

- • Take your excess "stuff" home.

- • Only frequently used items should be close to you.

The File Drawers

What to do:

- ❑ Step 1. Sort files by frequency of use. The less often touched, the farther away they should reside.

- ❑ Step 2. Label all files.

- ❑ Step 3. Clean out the contents of individual files, keeping only critical information.

Things to remember:

- Just because you inherited the files in your work space does not mean they should remain there.

- Thick files are better than thin ones. Consolidate related information.

Clearing the Top of Work Surfaces

What to do:

- ❑ Step 1. Start with one stack of papers and sort from the top down.

- ❑ Step 2. File items with related materials.

- ❑ Step 3. Put away completed work.

- ❑ Step 4. Place "hot" projects and tasks on your primary desk.

Things to remember:

- Separate reading items.

- Do not shuffle things you are not sure about, decide now.

REVIEW: GETTING ORGANIZED FROM A TO Z (continued)

Filing Guidelines

What to do:

❑ Step 1. Look at the files in your desk and credenza.

❑ Step 2. Decide which of these files should be very close and accessible.

❑ Step 3. Create working files for your current projects and your administrative activities.

❑ Step 4. Relabel, where necessary, keeping broad headings in mind.

❑ Step 5. Replace files in their proper locations immediately after use.

Filing Principles

What to do:

❑ Step 1. File papers in the broadest possible category.

❑ Step 2. Head files with a noun. Rarely, if ever, start with a date, number or adjective.

❑ Step 3. Alphabetize.

❑ Step 4. File articles by subject.

❑ Step 5. File and purge regularly.

Things to remember:

- Your files must be easy to use and should reduce the choices of where a document should live.

- When adding information, place the most current information in the front part of the file folder.

- Use your personal file for miscellaneous items that are of interest only to you.

- Use only alphabetic and subject headings for your personal files.

The Top of Your Desk

What to do:

- ❑ Step 1. Move all files to their proper locations.

- ❑ Step 2. Distribute all materials that go to others, get filed or go to storage.

- ❑ Step 3. Skim reading items and decide what to keep. If you keep an item, file it immediately with other related materials.

- ❑ Step 4. When you put things away place a note on your To-Do List, Master List, or Calendar.

- ❑ Step 5. Use a Project Monitoring Form to keep track of delegated projects.

Things to remember:

- Decisions may become more difficult but not impossible.

- Use an Out Box and clear the contents at least once a day.

- View the files in your desk drawer as being just as important as your phone, computer or writing implement: they should serve your needs.

REVIEW: GETTING ORGANIZED FROM A TO Z (continued)

Maintaining Your Organization

What to do:

❑ Step 1. Clear off your desk at the end of each day.

❑ Step 2. Be selective about what you keep.

❑ Step 3. Put things away; refile quickly.

Things to remember:

• Process each piece of paper as soon as it comes in.

• Ask three key questions to clear the In Box:

1. What does this refer to?

2. What is my next step?

3. What would I decide if it was one week before vacation?

• Jot notes where they belong initially, not on random little pieces of paper.

REVIEW: CLEARING THE TOP OF YOUR DESK

ITEM	PURPOSE	EXAMPLE	LOCATION
In Box	Single location to place newly arrived materials in preparation for	• Daily mail • Work from the Association • New information • Faxes	On your desk
Out Box	Single location for completed items prior to distribution.	• Response to letter delegated to Joe • Outgoing mail • Documents to type	On your desk
To-Do List	An ongoing list of things you are going to do. Serves as a memory aid and help to set priories.	• Phone calls to return • Evaluations to review • Letter to write • Work assignments to plan • Draft outline of program	On your desk
Calendar	Tells you *when* you will be completing or reviewing certain items. Should include due dates for projects.	• Upcoming meeting and its location • Appointments • Presentation dates • Hard deadlines	On your desk
Tickler File	For items needed in the future that do not have a permanent home elsewhere.	• Back-up documents for upcoming appointments • Application to fill out not due for six weeks • Items you will begin next week	With assistant or in the file drawer of the credenza

REVIEW: CLEARING THE TOP OF YOUR DESK (continued)

ITEM	PURPOSE	EXAMPLE	LOCATION
I. Working Files Current Projects	To keep documents pertaining to currently active projects together.	• The Anderson proposal • Quality improvement teams • Client files • Upcoming seminars	Inside your desk
II.Working Files Administrative Files	To keep documents pertaining to ongoing administrative projects or activities together.	• Minutes of weekly staff meetings • Newsletter ideas • Program descriptions • Financial information • Frequently used forms	Inside your desk
III. Working Files People Files	To hold information pertaining to people with whom you work closely. Any information where the next step in the process belongs to them.	• Note to check status of response • Paperwork related to new delegated project • Staff's long-term goals • Ideas to discuss next time you meet	Inside your desk
Wastebasket	To immediately remove unnecessary paper and to encourage quicker decision making.	• Anything that reads "you may have already won..." • Second copy of the semi-final draft of the preliminary...	Under your desk
Optional Reading File	To keep items for review off the desk, but not forgotten.	• Journals and magazines • Vendor newsletters • Articles	Credenza drawer

KEEP THE CLUTTER AWAY, PERMANENTLY

➤ Decide immediately. Commit yourself to making decisions now about what to do with each piece of paper.

➤ Ask yourself, "Do I really need it?" If so, file the document at once in the broadest category to which it refers.

➤ If possible, handle paper only once. When that is not possible, each time you touch a piece of paper, move it one step closer to completion.

➤ Do not set papers aside to decide later. If it must wait for a decision, place it in a Tickler File to return in one week. After that, make a decision.

➤ Spend fifteen minutes, twice a day, clearing out your In Box. Do not let it turn into a holding, aging, or procrastinating tray.

➤ Clear off the top of your desk at the end of your day. It completes the day's work, makes a clean space for you to see the next morning and stops paper build-up.

➤ Be realistic about the amount of information you can read and absorb. Limit the number of subscriptions you take, and clip articles as soon as you read them. Throw the rest of the periodical away or recycle it.

➤ Keep your organizing system and your files simple, easy and logical. Resist the desire to set up a mini Dewey decimal system or create some mythical "perfect" system.

➤ Purge your papers. Regular twice-a-year purges will keep the volume down. Whenever a file moves from active to inactive status, take the time to remove the unimportant notes, drafts and nonessential information.

➤ Break the habit of writing things down on numerous scraps of paper. Write notes in the appropriate place the first time.

➤ Sort incoming mail and e-mail into categories—by priority, by action, or by date.

CHECKLIST: MONITOR YOUR PROGRESS

After you complete your reorganizing project, check to see that you are maintaining your good habits. Once a month, for three months, and then every three months thereafter place a note on your calendar to monitor your progress. Particularly if you change locations, change jobs or experience a crisis that interrupts your normal work flow, be sure to review this checklist.

1. Do you have scraps of paper scattered on your desk?

   ❏ **Always**   ❏ **Sometimes**   ❏ **Never**

2. Do you clear your desk at the end of each day?

   ❏ **Always**   ❏ **Sometimes**   ❏ **Never**

3. Do you sort your mail with the waste basket close by?

   ❏ **Always**   ❏ **Sometimes**   ❏ **Never**

4. Do you have more than one pending stack?

   ❏ **Always**   ❏ **Sometimes**   ❏ **Never**

5. Are you able to retrieve items from your files quickly?

   ❏ **Always**   ❏ **Sometimes**   ❏ **Never**

6. Do you save most of the paper that crosses your desk?

   ❏ **Always**   ❏ **Sometimes**   ❏ **Never**

7. Do you use To-Do and Master Lists regularly?

   ❏ **Always**   ❏ **Sometimes**   ❏ **Never**

8. Are you comfortable with the follow-up procedures that you use?

❏ **Always**   ❏ **Sometimes**   ❏ **Never**

9. Do you purge your files regularly?

❏ **Always**   ❏ **Sometimes**   ❏ **Never**

10. Do you touch most papers only once before making a decision?

❏ **Always**   ❏ **Sometimes**   ❏ **Never**

11. Does the second desk or work table stay free of clutter?

❏ **Always**   ❏ **Sometimes**   ❏ **Never**

12. Are your files divided into logical groupings and alphabetized?

❏ **Always**   ❏ **Sometimes**   ❏ **Never**

13. Do you keep your reading stack low?

❏ **Always**   ❏ **Sometimes**   ❏ **Never**

14. Do you allot specific times during the day to respond to e-mail messages?

❏ **Always**   ❏ **Sometimes**   ❏ **Never**

15. Is your work space neat and comfortable to work in?

❏ **Always**   ❏ **Sometimes**   ❏ **Never**

SECTION

11

A Friendly Reminder

A FINAL WORD

Whether you have a processing system for your papers which needs some improvement, or you have a large amount of reorganizing to do, break it into small steps and it will go quickly. You have actually done a lot of the work in your head while you have been reading. *Organizing Your Work Space* has given you the tools and techniques you need. You do not need to spend lots of money on new "things," systems, software or color-coordinated equipment. Keep it simple and start now.

Organization is a living, breathing process. As your situation changes, so will your needs for ways to manage your paper. No matter what adaptations you may eventually require, the basic principles will always remain the same.

1. Throw out or recycle as much as possible.

2. Decide immediately; do not shuffle papers or create stacks.

3. Place like things together.

4. Label files and binders using broad, simple headings.

5. Keep close to you only the things you use frequently.

6. Complete items once you begin.

7. Make follow-up notes on a Calendar, Master List or To-Do List only.

8. Refile and replace things quickly.

9. Keep it simple.

10. Clear your desk at the end of each day.

A FINAL WORD (continued)

If you feel anxious during this rearranging process, understand that change is emotionally difficult. The fear that rises is normal. But do not let that fear immobilize you. Being disorganized is simply a habit that needs to be broken and replaced with one that is more effective.

Keep focused and you will begin to experience the benefits of being organized.

- More control

- Freedom from chaos

- More energy

- Freedom to be more creative

- Admiration from others

Yes, you can get organized and this will work for you. You deserve an organized work environment. Good luck!

BIBLIOGRAPHY

Aslett, Don. *Clutter Free! Finally and Forever.* Cincinnati: Marsh Creek Press, 1995.

Booher, Dianna. *Cutting Paperwork in the Corporate Culture.* New York: Facts on File Publications, 1986.

Culp, Stephanie. *Conquering the Paper Pile-Up.* Cincinnati: Writer's Digest Books, 1990.

Dorff, Pat. *File…Don't Pile!* New York: St. Martin's Press, 1983.

Hemphill, Barbara. *Taming the Office Tiger.* Washington: Kiplinger Times Business, 1996.

Hemphill, Barbara. *Taming the Paper Tiger: Organizing the Paper in Your Life.* New York: Dodd, Mead & Company, 1988.

Kanarek, Lisa. *Organizing Your Home Office for Success.* New York: Penguin Books, 1993.

Lehmkuhl, Dorothy and Lamping, Dolores Cotter. *Organizing for the Creative Person.* New York: Crown, 1993.

Lively, Lynn. *Managing Information Overload.* New York: AMACOM, 1996

Pollar, Odette. *365 Ways to Simplify Your Work Life.* Chicago: Dearborn Trade, 1996.

Ricks, Betty R. and Kay F. Gow. *Information Resource Management.* Florence, KY: South-Western Publishing Company, 1988.

Silver, Susan. *Organized to Be the Best!* Los Angeles: Adams-Hill Publishing, 1995.

Winston, Stephanie. *The Organized Executive.* New York: W. W. Norton & Company, 1983.

Association of Records Managers and Administrators (ARMA International)
4200 Somerset, Suite 215
Prairie Village, KS 66208
(913) 341-3808

Organizing Your Work Space

FOR MORE INFORMATION AND HELP

The National Association of
Professional Organizers
1033 La Posada Drive, Ste. 220
Austin, Texas 78752-3880
512-454-8626
FAX 512-454-3036

The Association of Records Managers
and Administrators
(ARMA International)
4200 Somerset, Ste. 215
Prairie Village, KS 66208
913-341-3808

Your Feedback Is Important!

This book is the result of feedback from many clients and from hundreds of people in training workshops and seminars. Your reactions to this book are very important. Please help by providing some feedback.

What was helpful about this book?

_____
_____
_____

Where can you see areas for improvement?

_____
_____
_____

Any additional comments?

_____
_____
_____
_____
_____

Thank you for taking the time to respond. Please mail, fax, or e-mail this form to:

Odette Pollar
TIME MANAGEMENT SYSTEMS
1441 Franklin Street, Suite 301
Oakland, CA 94612
1-800-599-TIME
Fax 510-763-0790
E-mail Opollartms@aol.com

Now Available From

Books • Videos • CD-ROMs • Computer-Based Training Products

If you enjoyed this book, we have great news for you. There are over 200 books available in the *Crisp Fifty-Minute™ Series*.
For more information contact

NETg
25 Thomson Place
Boston, MA 02210
1-800-442-7477
www.courseilt.com

Subject Areas Include:

Management
Human Resources
Communication Skills
Personal Development
Sales/Marketing
Finance
Coaching and Mentoring
Customer Service/Quality
Small Business and Entrepreneurship
Training
Life Planning
Writing

VERN